The Mayan Hermetic Brotherhood

A. S. Raleigh

THE MAYA BROTHERHOOD.

The Red Atlanteans who settled in Yucatan being members of the Hermetic Brotherhood of Atlantis, it followed naturally that the Brotherhood should be perpetuated among the Mayas. However, they gave a special trend to the Evolution of the Brotherhood such as it had never had in Atlantis. To them the all important Divine Principle was the Mother of the Gods, or the Great Mother, Female Vigor par excellence. This was quite natural for a people expressing that particular degree of Spirituality. They were no longer on the plane where they could adequately understand the Mystery of the Heart of Heaven or even its lowest aspect, Kosmic Thought. To them the all-important Mystery was that of the Generation of the Kosmos, hence the beginning of Kosmogenesis was the subject of their deepest veneration. Taking a somewhat practical view of the matter, it was not so much the Energy which was the Ultimate expression of this process as the Substance which molded and gave expression and form to the Kosmos. This being the case, it was inevitable that they should look more to the principle of Kosmic Motherhood that engendered the first manifestations of evolving life. It was not the Ultimate or Primordial World, the World of Ideas, that they were interested in, but rather the World of Form, of which they were a part. However, it must not be understood by this that they reverenced the Physical World, for that would be misleading; it was rather the realm of causation that eventuated in the Sensible World. It was not the Unmanifest, but rather the Manifestation, that they worshiped, but at the same time it was the Process of Manifestation rather than the Manifested State.

The Great Mother is the Molding Process which is ever going on in the Akasa, thus giving Form to it, and at the same time continually reforming it. She is not that which has given birth to the Universe, but rather that which is ever giving birth to it. This perpetual rebirth is made possible owing to the perpetual transformation that is going on all the time. Nothing is ever perfected, but rather every moment of time

is the Process of the Ever Becoming. The Great
Mother is at every moment of time bringing into manifestation that which is her own state of attainment at
that particular moment. When we realize that this
activity in the Female Vigor, or Kosmic Substance, en-
genders a state of Consciousness which is the Intelli-
gent aspect of that very state of activity—and thus she
is Self-Conscious with a Self-Consciousness exactly
corresponding to the State of Activity going on within
her—we can realize that this Self-Consciousness reacts
upon her Substance so as to determine the Mode of its
Activity, and thus the nature of the Formative process
which it will express. Therefore this Mother Substance is ever transforming itself, so that it becomes
the realization of its previous state of Self-Consciousness. This, therefore, means that It is evolving Itself.
At the same time that it does this, it is giving form to
its own Substance and thus is giving birth to certain
Modes of Activity, which are in reality specializations
of this very Substance, and which constitute the first
beginnings of Manifest Existence. It is thus that the
Great Mother is ever giving Birth to a Universe which
at the moment of its birth is the exact expression of
the Consciousness of the Great Mother, and yet in the
very act of giving Birth to that Universe the Substance
of the Great Mother has gone through a Transformation which has made her a slight degree in advance of
the Universe she has given birth to. Her experience of
Motherhood is therefore the means of her Evolution.
Not only is this true, but this new Mode of Activity,
with its accompanying Self-Consciousness, acts upon
the Substance of the Form which she has given Birth
to, so that it is transformed in accordance with the new
state of the Great Mother, and thus it is procreated
and born again in accordance with that new state.
From this it will be seen that the Universe is every
moment being reborn and also is at all times gestating
in the Womb of the Great Mother. The Substance of
the Great Mother is ever taking Form as the Universe,
and at the same time being resolved back into the state
of the Great Mother. The question then is, How can
the same Substance be at one and the same time the
Great Mother of the Universe and likewise the Universe itself? This becomes plain when we bear in mind

that the Great Mother is not a certain quantity of Substance separate from all other Substance, but is rather the Formative Molding process within Substance, the Universe being the Form which it takes at any given moment. To make the matter a little clearer, the Great Mother is the Tendency to Mold, while the Universe is the Process of being Molded. It is this distinction alone which marks the separation of the Universe from the Great Mother who is ever engendering it.

As a result of this Formative Activity of the Great Mother, there are certain specialized Modes of Activity which are in reality but so many differentiations of that Formative Process. Each one of these specialized Modes of Activity preserves its own identity with reference to every other such Mode, and yet the Formative Activity of the Great Mother so specialized is ever changing, so that the same transformation that is going on in the Great Mother Process is also going on in her Modes, so that there is in these Modes of Activity a Creative Evolutionary Process exactly analogous to that which is going on in the Great Mother herself. These specialized Modes of Activity are called the Gucumatz, the Serpents with Dazzling Azure Wings. These Gucumatz are the Kundalini Forces of the Kosmos, or the Creative Fires, hence the Fiery Serpents of the Mysteries. They are likewise the Gestative Fires in the Womb of the Great Mother. They are all specialized manifestations of the Kosmic Fire. It is these Forces which are spoken of as the Fires of the Universe, that is, the Fires out of which the Universe is engendered. They are the Consuming Fire of Rider Haggard, the Rosicrucian Fire, the Fire of the Heart of Nature, the Fire of Life and likewise the Fire Mist of Science. The Sacred Fire of the Temple was the Symbol of those Serpents of Fire, each Fire symbolizing one of the Fiery Serpents. Likewise are the Altar Lamps their symbols, except in the case where they symbolize the Lights which have either a higher or a lower meaning than the Creative Fires. The Sacred Fire was never permitted to go out for the reason that the Gucumatz must never cease their life of Perpetual Mutation. The Sacred Fires were attended by Virgins whose duty it was to tend the Sacred Fire and see that it never went out. They were women for the reason that the Gucumatz were the Creative Fires of the Great Mother, and, as they were Feminine, they must be tended by women. The meaning of this was that in the Kosmos it was the Mother Principle of the Great Mother acting through them that ever renewed them and kept them burning. They were virgins for the reason that, having never known a man, they were the fit symbol of the Feminine Essence of the Great Mother that was expressing itself in that way. They were not Masculine Fires, but, from the Maya conception, Feminine Fires, and were but the modes of manifestation of that Mothering process. Another thing that was symbolized here was the application of this Mystery to the Individual. In this sense, the Guardian of the Sacred Fire was feeding it within her own soul, and in this sense she must be a virgin, for only by the conservation of the Feminine Sex Magnetism could the Fire of the Soul be kept burning, and thus the lower nature be ever regenerated. The Keeper of the Sacred Fire dressd in a special manner. She wore a loose Loin Cloth or skirt falling from the waist to a point just above the knees, and a Sacrificial Apron over the front part of the body from the waist to a point just high enough to cover the breasts. The Loin Cloth was Green, to symbolize the Earth, for water is the symbol of the Feminine Substance wherever it may be found. When water has descended in the form of rain and has watered the earth, it causes the earth to bring forth vegetation, which is in reality water in the form of vegetation. This is Green in color and covers the earth with a mantle of Green, hence in this sense Green is the symbol of the Mother Principle manifesting through Physical Matter. For this reason Green symbolizes Water wherever it may be found. The Green Skirt is therefore the symbol of the Mother Principle in the Earth. Also the figure from the waist down is the symbol of the Earth, while from the waist up it symbolizes the Sky, or that which is above the Physical Plane. The Green Cloth covers all of that part of the body suggesting Generation, which indicates that the Sacred Fires are lost in the generation of matter, and therefore are not Fire but Water on that plane. Blue is the color of the Sky, and hence is the symbol of the Airy Region between the Water and the Fire. This covers those parts of the body that are connected with the elements of Motherhood above the waist line; that is, according to the mysteries, in the Airy Region. The locality of the Womb and Uterus as well as the Breasts, which are associated with the nursing of the child after birth, are covered with the Apron of Air. The meaning of this is that as the Gucumatz are Fiery, they cease to be the Gucumatz as soon as they pass below the level of the Fire, and therefore they become something else. These Sacred Fires do not Generate on those planes, but rather they engender that which generates there. Again, they are not in reality the Generatrix, but are the modes of Generation of the Generatrix. The penalty for permitting the Sacred Fires to go out is death, for if the Gucumatz were to cease to operate the Universe would cease to be, and if those Fires die out in the Soul the soul will cease to be.

The Gucumatz in their activity tend to the production of Unity of Action. Out of the totality of their specialized activities there is born a synthesized activity making for Unity. This united activity results in a living, active, self-conscious, creative process. A process that is ever changing, yet ever the same, for it is the consequence of the united action of the Gucumatz. This is the Synthesized Fire resulting from the synthetic action of all the diverse Creative Fires. It is the Process of the Ever Becoming in the absolute sense. This is the Universe, as the Child of the Great Mother, the Child that is ever being born, and at the same time ever Gestating in the Womb of the Great Mother, for it is at once the synthesis of the Fires and that which results from the synthesis. It is at once the Creative Evolutionary Process and also that which is Created and Evolved. This is Kukulkan, or the Feathered Serpent. The Serpent represents the Fire and the Feathers the Air. Thus the Feathered Serpent is this Creative Evolutionary Process, or rather the Form which it assumes on the Plane of Fire and Air. The Azure Wings of the Gucumatz also represent the element of Air, and the meaning is that the Gucumatz are merged and lost in the Feathered Serpent. In a word, they cease to be the Gucumatz and become the Feathered Serpent, or the Universe. The Feathered Serpent is supposed to be Masculine, though in reality he in-

cludes the Feminine element within himself. He is the
Universe above the Physical Plane. In the latter He
becomes in a great measure Fixed, so that the form
changes again.

On the Physical Plane or, to speak more accurately,
in the Etheric Region, the forces of the Feathered Serpent take a more stable form and become the Great
Macow Bird that descends from the Heavens to the
Earth. This great Macow Bird is the Universe in the
form of Physical Ether, and is the Fabricator that, out
of its own nature, fabricates the World of Gross Matter. This Principle is both Male and Female, having
the two sexes in a state of balance. It is but the expression of the Feathered Serpent on the Physical Octave.

The activities of the Great Macow become fixed in
Votan, the Gross Physical Universe, but as this is but
the fabricated result of the Fabricating Process going
on in the Great Macow it follows that the Earth, or
Votan, is in a process of continual change, or Evolution.

The Great Macow was the Patron Goddess of the
Queen, for the reason that the Queen was supposed
to embody the Feminine aspect of the Fabricator, and
to be the Fabricatrix of the Nation, therefore her
Totem was the Macow, just as the National Standard
was the Feathered Serpent. The meaning of this latter symbolism was that the Mayas as a people must
change as the Feathered Serpent changed, and must in
fact at all times ensoul the Feathered Serpent at that
particular moment; thus they must evolve with the
Universe. Therefore the Mayas were, to all intents
and purposes, the Universe.

When the High Priest went into the Sanctuary to
consult the gods he always went naked, for in their
presence he was not a priest but a supplicant. He was,
in fact, the representative of the people, and stood in
their presence devoid of all covering and of all orna-
ment, for he must bring his naked soul to them if he
was to know their will. When he went forth to de-
clare the will of the gods to the people, he went as the
representative of the gods, whom all must obey, hence
he was the High Priest, and therefore he dressed in all
his Sacerdotal Vestments, as became the messenger of
the Gods.

They offered human sacrifices, and in this way symbolized the fact that it is only by dying on the Plane of the Manifested that we can return to the Bosom of the Divine Mother. This Rite also taught that those who thus die on the lower planes and enter the state of the Great Mother exercise a Vicarious influence on human life below, thus tending to lift the Race Spirit up in the direction of the Great Mother. It was never believed there was any Vicarious efficacy in the Sacrifice itself; it was rather the idea of symbolizing in the form of a sacrificial death on the Physical Plane the Mystic Death, or Living Death, of the Sacred Person who undertook to kill out the Generative Processes that were going on in him below the level of the Great Mother. As this was a symbol of the Mystic Death, few Human Sacrifices were offered, only enough to keep the Idea of Vicarious Living Sacrifice alive in the consciousness of the people. It may be farther stated that in the original Mayan Religion there were no Human Sacrifices, but only the Living Deaths, but as time went by they lost sight of the original meaning of the Mystery and began to symbolize it by the actual offering of Blood Sacrifices. This in time tended to some extent to hide the Spiritual Meaning of the Rite altogether.

Their Mysticism was largely Mathematical and Geometrical in its Symbolism. Their most Sacred Numbers were 3, 5, 7, 9 and 13. The meaning of these Numbers will be clear to all who are versed in Occult Mathematics and will unveil the inner meaning of much of their Mysteries as well as their Hieroglyphics. Nine is the number of the Hermetic Ogdoad with Kosmic Thought or Thoth at the head of it. With the Mayas this position was occupied by the Heart of Heaven as the First, the Father and the Mother of the Gods as the Second and Third, the Feathered Serpent polarized as Male and Female as the Fourth and Fifth, the Great Macow, both male and female, as Sixth and Seventh, and Votan polarized as male and female as Eighth and Ninth. Nine was also the number of Gestation of the Foetus and therefore symbolized the Gestation and Birth of the Feathered Serpent.

CPSIA information can be obtained
at www.ICGtesting.com
Printed in the USA
LVRC030738041020
667786LV00006BC/27